How is the Weather?

by Jim Collins

Glenview, Illinois • Boston, Massachusetts • Chandler, Arizona
Upper Saddle River, New Jersey

umbrella

It is raining. Some people do not have umbrellas!

They did not know it would rain. They were surprised.

How can you find out about the weather?

thermometer

beach ball

This family wants to go to the park. Is the temperature right for a day in the park?

The family looked at the thermometer outside their house. It is 70 degrees outside. It is a perfect day for a picnic!

This man is fishing at the beach. He is wearing a jacket because it is a cool day. He knew it would be cool outside because he listened to the weather forecast on TV.

---

weather forecast: a prediction that says what the weather will be

These players are waiting to play their soccer game. They cannot play soccer because it is raining.

The weather spoiled the team's plans. When will the rain stop? Will it be sunny later today?

hot air
balloon

It is a clear day. This family is going
for a special ride in a hot air balloon.
There are no clouds in the sky today.
It is a perfect day for a balloon ride. This
family listened to the weather forecast.

snow

These girls are wearing coats and gloves. It is cold outside. It snowed last night. There is no school today!

How deep is the snow? The girls have a ruler to measure the new snow.

On warm days we can go to the pool.

On cold days we can sit by a warm fire.

It is important to know what the weather will be.

What is the forecast for tomorrow?